SpringerBriefs in Computer Science

W0225716

Series Editors

Stan Zdonik
Peng Ning
Shashi Shekhar
Jonathan Katz
Xindong Wu
Lakhmi C. Jain
David Padua
Xuemin Shen
Borko Furht
V. S. Subrahmanian
Martial Hebert
Katsushi Ikeuchi
Bruno Siciliano

For further volumes:
http://www.springer.com/series/10028

Xuxian Jiang · Yajin Zhou

Android Malware

 Springer

Xuxian Jiang
Yajin Zhou
North Carolina State University
Raleigh, NC
USA

ISSN 2191-5768   ISSN 2191-5776 (electronic)
ISBN 978-1-4614-7393-0   ISBN 978-1-4614-7394-7 (eBook)
DOI 10.1007/978-1-4614-7394-7
Springer New York Heidelberg Dordrecht London

Library of Congress Control Number: 2013938162

Printed on acid-free paper

Springer is part of Springer Science+Business Media (www.springer.com)

For Matthew, Grace, and Rainna

Acknowledgments

This book is based on our years-long research conducted to systematically analyze emerging Android malware. Some of our earlier research results and findings were reported in an IEEE conference paper entitled *Dissecting Android Malware*: *Characterization and Evolution*, which was presented at the IEEE Symposium on Security and Privacy (often mentioned as Oakland conference in the security community) in May, 2012 [77]. During and after the conference, we were pleased to receive and hear inquiries from colleagues with encouraging comments on the systematization of knowledge work that has been conducted in our conference paper. Partially because of that, we are motivated to expand our work and hope such efforts will be of service to the security and privacy community. Further, as part of that, we have released corresponding malware dataset for our study under the name *Android Malware Genome Project* to the community.

With that, we want to take this opportunity to thank our collaborators, Dongyan Xu, Peng Ning, Xinyuan Wang, Shihong Zou, and others, whose valuable insights and comments greatly enriched our work. The authors are also grateful to colleagues in the Cyber Defense Lab at NC State University, especially Tyler Bletsch, Zhi Wang, Michael Grace, Deepa Srinivasan, Minh Q. Tran, Chiachih Wu, Wu Zhou, and Kunal Patel. Special thanks also go to Susan Lagerstrom-Fife and our publisher for their great help and patience!

This research was supported in part by the US National Science Foundation (NSF) under Grants 0855297, 0855036, 0910767, and 0952640. Any opinions, findings, and conclusions or recommendations expressed in this material are those of the authors and should not be interpreted as necessarily representing the official policies or endorsements, either expressed or implied, for the NSF.

Contents

Acronyms

ACM	Association for Computing Machinery
AES	Advanced Encryption Standard
AOSP	Android Open Source Project
API	Application Programming Interface
ASLR	Address Space Layout Randomization
C&C	Command and Control
CCS	Computer and Communications Security
CNN	Cable News Network
DES	Data Encryption Standard
DRM	Digital Rights Management
DVM	Dalvik Virtual Machine
HTML	Hypertext Markup Language
HTTP	Hypertext Transfer Protocol
IMEI	International Mobile Equipment Identity
J2ME	Java 2 Platform Micro Edition
JAR	Java Archive
JNI	Java Native Interface
MMS	Multimedia Messaging Service
OS	Operating System
PC	Personal Computer
QR Code	Quick Response Code
SHA1	Secure Hashing Algorithm 1
SIM	Subscriber Identification Module
SMS	Short Message Service
SQL	Structured Query Language
SSL	Secure Sockets Layer
UI	User Interface
URL	Uniform Resource Locator
WAP	Wireless Application Protocol
WIFI	Wireless Fidelity
XN	eXecute Never

Chapter 1
Introduction

Recent years have witnessed an explosive growth in smartphone sales and adoption. According to CNN [39], smartphone shipments have tripled in the past three years from 40 million to about 120 million. The year of 2011 even marks as the first time in history that smartphones have outsold personal computers. Unfortunately, the increasing adoption of smartphones comes with the growing prevalence of mobile malware. As the most popular mobile platform, Google's Android overtook others (e.g., Symbian) to become the top mobile malware platform. A recent Kaspersky report [22] highlights that "among all mobile malware, the share of Android-based malware is higher than 46 % and still growing rapidly." Another similar report from Juniper Networks [17] also alerts that there is "400 percent increase in Android-based malware since summer 2010."

Recognizing the rampant growth of Android malware, this book aims to de-mysterize emerging Android malware and present a systematic characterization of them. One main purpose here is to help readers to gain an in-depth understanding of Android malware so that an effective mitigation solution can be practically developed and deployed. In addition, we realize that the community is largely constrained by the lack of a comprehensive mobile malware dataset to start with. To change that and also engage the research community to better our understanding and defense, we accordingly release our dataset to the community under the name *Android Malware Genome Project* [1] Our dataset so far contains 1260 Android malware samples (with distinct SHA1 values) in 49 different Android malware families and covers the majority of existing Android malware, ranging from their debut in August 2010 to recent ones in October 2011. The dataset is made possible from more than one year effort in collecting related malware samples, including manual or automated crawling from a number of Android marketplaces.

Based on the collected malware samples, we perform a relatively comprehensive survey and aim to characterize these malware based on their detailed behavior

---

[1] The Android Malware Genome Project is accessible at http://www.malgenomeproject.org/. To prevent our dataset from being misused, we may require verifying user identity or request necessary justification before the dataset can be downloaded. More details will be described in Chap. 2.

X. Jiang and Y. Zhou, *Android Malware*, SpringerBriefs in Computer Science,
DOI: 10.1007/978-1-4614-7394-7_1, © The Author(s) 2013

break-down, including their installation methods, activation, and built-in malicious payloads. We believe such survey is instrumental to not only detecting possible outbreaks of certain Android malware in the wild, but also facilitating our understanding and shedding light on possible defenses.

As an example, from the collected 1260 malware samples, we find that 1083 of them (or 86.0 %) are repackaged versions of legitimate applications with malicious payloads, which indicates the policing need of detecting repackaged applications in the current Android marketplaces. Also, we observe that more recent Android malware families are adopting update attacks and drive-by downloads to infect users, which are more stealthy and difficult to detect. Further, when analyzing the carried payloads, we notice a number of alarming statistics: (1) Around one third (36.7 %) of the collected malware samples leverage root-level exploits to fully compromise the Android security, posing the highest level of threats to users' security and privacy; (2) More than 90 % communicate with remote servers and/or turn the compromised phones into a botnet controlled through network or short messages. (3) Among the 49 malware families, 28 of them (with 571 or 45.3 % samples) have the built-in support of sending out background short messages (to premium-rate numbers) or making phone calls without user awareness. (4) Last but not least, 27 malware families (with 644 or 51.1 % samples) are harvesting user's information, including user accounts and short messages stored on the phones.

Following the general survey of existing Android malware, we further zoom in on a few representative Android malware and study their evolution in the wild. We are amazed by their rapid evolution and uneasy to notice that existing anti-malware solutions are seriously lagging behind. For example, it is not uncommon for Android malware to have encrypted root exploits or obfuscated command and control (C&C) servers. The adoption of various sophisticated techniques greatly raises the bar for their detection. In addition, our zoom-in study shows that malware authors are quickly learning from each other to create hybrid threats. For example, one recent Android malware, i.e., *AnserverBot* [27] (reported in September 2011), is clearly inspired from *Plankton* [30] (reported in June 2011) to have the dynamic capability of fetching and executing payload at runtime, posing significant challenges for the development of next-generation anti-mobile-malware solutions.

The rest of this book is organized as follows: Chap. 2 presents a survey on existing Android malware in the wild, including detailed timeline analysis and behavioral break-down of their infection. After that, Chap. 3 presents several case studies on representative Android malware samples as well as their evolution in the wild. Chapter 4 discusses possible ways for future improvement. In this book, while we aim to make it accessible to those new to the area, we do not intend to provide a comprehensive tutorial on various aspects of Android malware. Instead, we refer the interested readers to various references and additional readings, particularly those highlighted in Chap. 5 Lastly, we summarize this book in Chap. 6.

Chapter 2
A Survey of Android Malware

In this chapter, we present a survey of existing Android malware. Particularly, with more than one year effort, we have collected a large dataset of existing Android malware. Based on this dataset, we are able to systematically characterize existing Android malware from various aspects, including their installation, activation methods, and malicious payloads.

2.1 Malware Dataset

When the very first Android malware, i.e., the *FakePlayer* malware [28], was discovered in August 2010, we realized the importance of collecting them for systematic examination. Specifically, to that end, we take two main approaches to actively collect Android malware samples. The first one is to obtain relevant information of new Android malware by following up with any Android malware announcements, threat reports, and event blog contents from existing mobile anti-virus companies and active researchers [8, 13, 16, 21, 31, 32] as exhaustively as possible and then diligently requesting malware samples from them. The second one is to crawl malware samples directly from existing Android marketplaces, including both third-party and official Android Market.[1]

With more than one year effort (i.e., from August 2010 to October 2011), we have successfully collected 1260 Android malware samples in 49 malware families. In Fig. 2.1, we show the list of the 49 Android malware families in our dataset along with the time when each particular malware family is discovered. If we take a look at the Android malware history [23] from the very first Android malware *FakePlayer* in August 2010 to recent ones in October 2011, it spans slightly more than one year with around 52 Android malware families reported. Our dataset so far has 1260 samples in 49 different malware families, indicating a very decent coverage of existing Android malware.

---

[1] Android Market is now part of Google Play.

X. Jiang and Y. Zhou, *Android Malware*, SpringerBriefs in Computer Science, DOI: 10.1007/978-1-4614-7394-7_2, © The Author(s) 2013

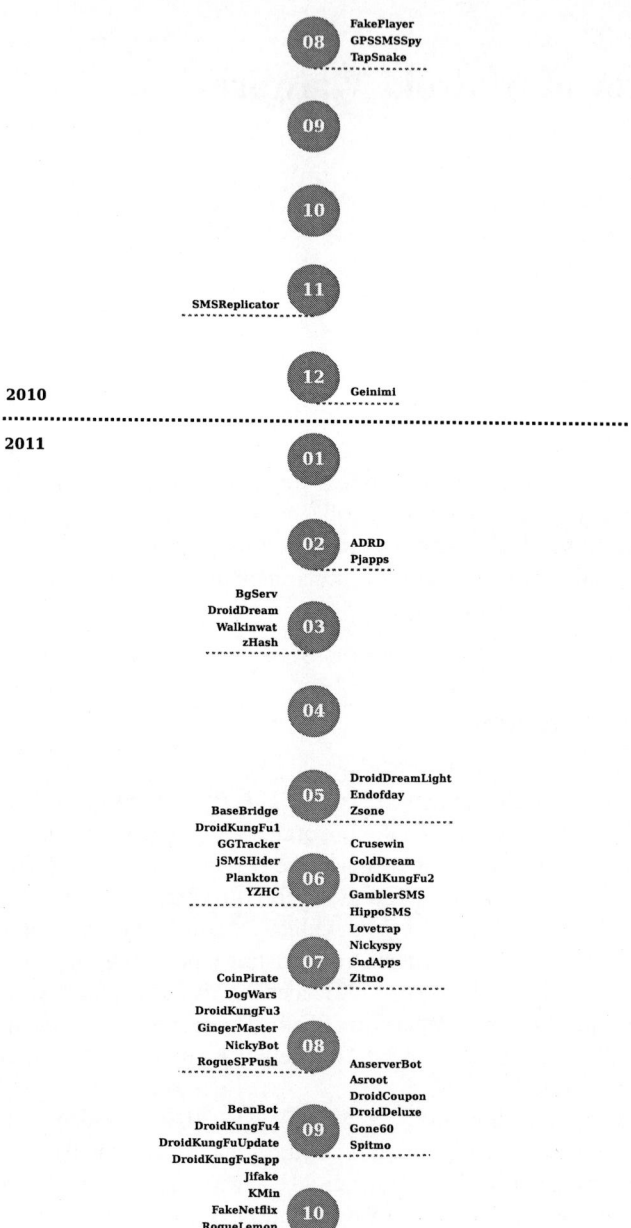

Fig. 2.1 The timeline of 49 Android malware families in our study

To engage the research community and better our defense, we released this dataset in May 2012 to community under the name *Android Malware Genome Project*. Immediately following the release, we received numerous requests and have so far

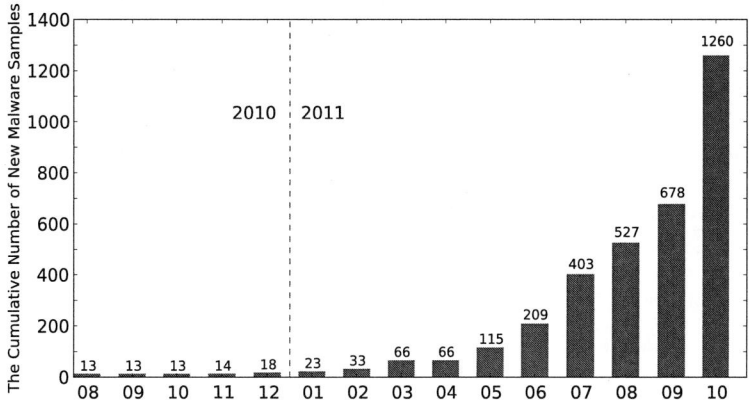

Fig. 2.2 The cumulative growth of new malware samples in our collection

shared our dataset with more than 160 universities, research labs and companies from five continents (except Antarctica) across the world. We have the reason to believe that the earlier efforts of sample collection, analysis, and sharing are useful to the community and therefore are motivated to continue to do so.

In order to characterize Android malware growth in the wild, we show the monthly cumulative growth of Android malware in Fig. 2.2. The figure clearly indicates that starting summer 2011, Android malware has experienced an exponential growth. The outbreaks of several major Android malware families, such as *DroidKungFu* (June, 2011) and *AnserverBot* (September, 2011), greatly contribute to the trend: among these 1260 samples in our dataset, 37.5 % of them are related to *DroidKungFu* [29] and its variants; 14.8 % are *AnserverBot* [27]. Most of these malicious apps are still actively evolving and we will have a detailed study of them in Chap. 3.

2.2 Malware Characterization

Based on the dataset, we next present a systematic characterization of existing Android malware. By doing so, we can possibly understand how they infect mobile users and what kinds of damage that might be caused. Also we will compare the list of permissions often requested by malware with popular benign apps (e.g., from official Android Market) and illustrate key differences between the two.

2.2.1 Malware Installation

To infect mobile users, malicious apps typically lure users into downloading and installing them. By manually analyzing them, we categorize their attack techniques into the following ones: *repackaging*, *update attack*, and *drive-by download*.

Repackaging is one of most widely-adopted techniques in Android malware, which basically works by first downloading popular benign apps, repackaging them with additional malicious payloads, and then uploading repackaged ones to various Android marketplaces. Update attack does not directly inject malicious payloads into benign apps. Instead, the malicious payloads are disguised as the "updated" version of legitimate apps. Drive-by download is similar to traditional web-based attack that is launched to redirect users to download malware, e.g., by using aggressive in-app advertisement or malicious QR code.

2.2.1.1 Repackaging

As mentioned earlier, repackaging is one of the most common techniques malware authors use to piggyback malicious payloads into popular apps. In essence, malware authors may locate and download popular apps, disassemble them, enclose malicious payloads, re-assemble and then submit the new apps to official and/or alternative Android markets. Users could be vulnerable by being enticed to download and install these infected apps.

To quantify the use of repackaging technique among our dataset, we take the following approach: if a sample shares the same package name with an app in the official Android Market, we then download the official app and manually compare the difference, which typically contains the malicious payload added by malware authors. If the original app is not available, we choose to disassemble the malware sample and manually determine whether the malicious payload is a natural part of the main functionality of the host app. If not, it is considered as repackaged app.

In total, among the 1260 malware samples, 1083 of them (or 86.0 %) are repackaged. By further classifying them based on each individual family (Table 2.1), we find that within the total 49 families in our collection, 25 of them infect users by these repackaged apps while 25 of them are standalone apps, which are designed to be spyware in the first place. One malware family, i.e., *GoldDream*, utilizes both for its infection. Among these repackaged apps, we find that malware authors have chosen a variety of apps for repackaging, including paid apps, popular game apps, powerful utility apps (including security updates), as well as porn-related apps. For instance, one *AnserverBot* malware sample repackaged a paid app *com.camelgames.mxmotor* available on the official Android Market and injected its malicious payload. Another *BgServ* [6] malware sample repackaged the security tool released by Google to remove *DroidDream* from infected phones.

Possibly due to the attempt to hide piggybacked malicious payloads, malware authors tend to use the class-file names which look legitimate and benign. For example, *AnserverBot* malware uses a package name *com.sec.android.provider.drm* for its payload, which looks like a module that provides legitimate DRM functionality. The first version of *DroidKungFu* chooses to use *com.google.ssearch* to disguise as the Google search module and its follow-up versions use *com.google.update* to pretend to be an official Google update.

Table 2.1 An overview of existing Android malware (Part I: installation and activation)

	Installation				Activation							
	Repackaging	Update	Drive-by download	Standalone	BOOT	SMS	NET	CALL	USB	PKG	BATT	SYS
ADRD	✓				✓		✓	✓				
AnserverBot	✓	✓			✓	✓	✓	✓	✓		✓	✓
Asroot				✓								
BaseBridge	✓	✓			✓	✓	✓				✓	✓
BeanBot	✓					✓		✓				
BgServ	✓				✓	✓						
CoinPirate	✓				✓	✓						
Crusewin				✓	✓	✓						
DogWars	✓											
DroidCoupon	✓				✓		✓	✓		✓		
DroidDeluxe				✓								
DroidDream	✓							✓				
DroidDreamLight	✓				✓							
DroidKungFu1	✓				✓						✓	✓
DroidKungFu2	✓				✓						✓	✓
DroidKungFu3	✓				✓						✓	✓
DroidKungFu4	✓				✓						✓	✓
DroidKungFuSapp	✓				✓							✓
DroidKungFuUpdate	✓	✓										
Endofday	✓				✓	✓						
FakeNetflix				✓								
FakePlayer				✓								
GamblerSMS				✓	✓							
Geinimi	✓				✓	✓						

(Continued)

Table 2.1 (Continued)

	Installation				Activation							
	Repackaging	Update	Drive-by download	Standalone	BOOT	SMS	NET	CALL	USB	PKG	BATT	SYS
GGTracker			✓	✓	✓	✓						
GingerMaster	✓				✓						✓	
GoldDream	✓			✓	✓	✓		✓				
Gone60				✓								
GPSSMSSpy	✓					✓						
HippoSMS	✓				✓							
Jifake			✓			✓						
jSMSHider	✓									✓		
KMin		✓										
Lovetrap				✓	✓	✓						
NickyBot				✓	✓	✓						
Nickyspy				✓	✓							
Pjapps	✓			✓	✓	✓						✓
Plankton				✓								
RogueLemon				✓		✓						
RogueSPPush				✓		✓						
SMSReplicator				✓		✓						
SndApps				✓								
Spitmo			✓	✓	✓	✓		✓				
TapSnake				✓	✓							
Walkinwat				✓								
YZHC				✓	✓							
zHash			✓		✓							
Zitmo						✓						
Zsone	✓					✓						

It is interesting to note that one malware family— *jSMSHider* —uses a publicly available private key (serial number: *b3998086d056cffa*) that is distributed in the Android Open Source Project (AOSP). The current Android security model allows the apps signed with the same platform key of the phone firmware to request the permissions which are otherwise not available to normal third-party apps. One such permission includes the installation of additional apps without user intervention. Unfortunately, a few (earlier) popular custom firmware images were signed by the default key distributed in AOSP. As a result, the *jSMSHider*-infected apps may obtain privileged permissions to perform dangerous operations (installing another app which can send SMS messages to premium-rate numbers) without user's awareness.

2.2.1.2 Update Attack

The first technique typically piggybacks the entire malicious payloads into host apps, which could potentially expose their presence. The second technique makes it difficult for detection. Specifically, it may still repackage popular apps. But instead of enclosing the payload as a whole, it only includes an update component that will fetch or download the malicious payloads at runtime. As a result, static scanning of host apps may fail to capture the malicious payloads. In our dataset, there are four malware families, i.e., *BaseBridge*, *DroidKungFuUpdate*, *AnserverBot*, and *Plankton*, that adopt this attack (Table 2.1).

The *BaseBridge* malware has a number of variants. While some embed root exploits that allow for silent installation of additional apps without user intervention, we here focus on other variants that use the update attacks without root exploits. Specifically, when a *BaseBridge*-infected app runs, it will check whether an update dialogue needs to be displayed. If yes, by essentially saying that a new version is available, the user will be offered to install the updated version (Fig. 2.3a) (The new version is actually stored in the host app as a resource or asset file). If the user accepts, an "updated" version with the malicious payload will then be installed (Fig. 2.3b). Because the malicious payload is in the "updated" app, *not* the original app itself, it is more stealthy than the first technique that directly includes the entire malicious payload in the first place.

The *DroidKungFuUpdate* malware is similar to *BaseBridge*. But instead of carrying or enclosing the "updated" version inside the original app, it chooses to remotely download a new version from network. Moreover, it takes a stealthy route by notifying the users through a third-party library [35] that provides the (legitimate) notification functionality. (Note the functionality is similar to the automatic notification from the Google's Cloud to Device Messaging framework.) Once downloaded, the "updated" version turns out to be the *DroidKungFu3* malware. By leveraging the service provided by legitimate library to download Android malware, it becomes stealthy and hard to detect.

The previous two update attacks require user approval to download and install new versions. Others such as *AnserverBot* and *Plankton* advance the update attack by stealthily upgrading certain components in the host apps *not* the entire app. As a

(a)   **(b)**

Fig. 2.3 An update attack from *BaseBridge*. **a** The update dialog. **b** Installation of a new version

result, it does not require user approval. In particular, *Plankton* directly fetches and runs a *JAR* file maintained in a remote server while *AnserverBot* retrieves a public (encrypted) blog entry, which contains the actual payloads for update! Apparently, the stealthy nature of these update attacks poses significant challenges for their detection. We will analyze these two malware families in Chap. 3.

2.2.1.3 Drive-by Download

The third technique applies the traditional drive-by download attacks to mobile space. Though they are not directly exploiting mobile browser vulnerabilities, they are essentially enticing users to download "interesting" or "feature-rich" apps. In our collection, we have four such malware families, i.e., *GGTracker* [14], *Jifake* [18], *Spitmo* [12] and *ZitMo* [37]. The last two are designed to steal user's sensitive banking information.

The *GGTracker* malware starts from in-app advertisements. In particular, when a user clicks a special advertisement link, it will redirect the user to a malicious website, which claims to be analyzing the battery usage of user's phone and will redirect the user to a fake Android Market to download an app (for the purpose of improving battery efficiency). Unfortunately, the downloaded app is not one that focuses on improving the efficiency of battery, but a malware that will subscribe to a premium-rate service without user's knowledge.

Similarly, the *Jifake* malware is downloaded when users are redirected to a malicious website. However, it is not using in-app advertisements to attract and redirect users. Instead, it uses a malicious QR code [24], which when scanned will redirect the user to another URL containing the *Jifake* malware. This malware itself is the repackaged mobile ICQ client, which sends several SMS messages to a premium-rate number. While QR code-based malware propagation has been warned earlier [34], this is the first time that this attack actually occurred in the wild.

The last two *Spitmo* and *ZitMo* are ported versions of nefarious PC malware, i.e., *SpyEye* and *Zeus*. They work in a similar manner: when a user is doing online banking with a comprised PC, the user will be redirected to download a particular smartphone app, which is claimed to better protect online banking activities. However, the downloaded app is actually a malware, which can collect and send mTANs (a credential for online banking) or SMS messages to a remote server. These two malware families rely on the comprised desktop browsers to launch the attack. Though it may seem hard to infect real users, the fact that they can steal sensitive bank information raises serious alerts to users.

2.2.1.4 Others

We have so far presented three main social engineering-based techniques that have been used in existing Android malware. Next, we examine the rest samples that do not fall in the above three categories. In particular, our dataset has 1083 repackaged apps, which leaves 177 standalone apps. We therefore look into those standalone apps and organize them into the following four groups.

The first group is considered spyware as claimed by themselves—they intend to be installed to victim's phones on purpose. That probably explains why attackers have no motivations or the need to lure victim for installation. *GPSSMSSpy* is an example that listens to SMS-based commands to record and upload the victim's current location.

The second group includes those fake apps that masquerade as the legitimate apps but stealthily perform malicious actions, such as stealing users' credentials or sending background SMS messages. *FakeNetflix* is an example that steals a user's Netflix account and password. Note that it is not a repackaged version of Netflix app but instead disguises to be *the* Netflix app with the same user interface. *FakePlayer* is another example that masquerades as a movie player but does not provide the advertised functionality at all. All it does is to send SMS messages to premium-rate numbers without user awareness.

The third group contains apps that also intentionally include malicious functionality (e.g., sending unauthorized SMS messages or subscribing to some value-added services automatically). But the difference from the second group is that they are not fake ones. Instead, they can provide the functionality they claimed. But unknown to users, they also include certain malicious functionality. For example, one *RogueSPPush* sample is an astrology app. But it will automatically subscribe to premium-rate services by intentionally hiding and automatically replying to subscription-confirming SMS messages.

The last group includes those apps that rely on the root privilege to function well. However, without asking the user to grant the root privilege to these apps, they leverage known root exploits to escape from the built-in security sandbox. Though these apps may not clearly demonstrate malicious intents, the fact of using root exploits without user permission seems cross the line. Examples in this group include *Asroot* and *DroidDeluxe*.

2.2.2 Activation

Next, we examine the system-wide Android events of interest to existing Android malware. By registering for the related system-wide events, Android malware can rely on the built-in support of automated event notification and callbacks on Android to flexibly trigger or launch its payloads. For simplicity, we abbreviate some frequently-used Android events in Table 2.2 (and use them in Table 2.1).

Among all available system events, *BOOT_COMPLETED* is the most interested one to existing Android malware. This is not surprising as this particular event will be triggered when the system finishes its booting process—a perfect timing for malware to kick off its background services. By listening to this event, the malware can start

Table 2.2 The (abbreviated) Android events/actions of interest to existing malware

Abbreviation	Events	Abbreviation	Events
BOOT (Boot Completed)	BOOT_COMPLETED	SMS (SMS/MMS)	SMS_RECEIVED WAP_PUSH_RECEIVED
CALL (Phone Events)	PHONE_STATE NEW_OUTGOING _CALL	USB (USB Storage)	UMS_CONNECTED UMS_DISCONNECTED
PKG (Package)	PACKAGE_ADDED PACKAGE_REMOVED PACKAGE_CHANGED	BATT (Power/ Battery)	ACTION_POWER_CONNECTED ACTION_POWER _DISCONNECTED
	PACKAGE_REPLACED PACKAGE_RESTARTED PACKAGE_INSTALL		BATTERY_LOW BATTERY_OKAY BATTERY_CHANGED_ACTION
SYS (System Events)	USER_PRESENT INPUT_METHOD _CHANGED SIG_STR SIM_FULL	NET (Network)	CONNECTIVITY_CHANGE PICK_WIFI_WORK

itself without user's intervention. In our dataset, 29 (with 83.3 % of the samples) malware families listen to this event.

The *SMS_RECEIVED* comes second with 21 malware families interested in it. This event will be broadcasted to the whole system when a new SMS message is being received. By listening to this event, the malware can be keen in intercepting or responding to particular incoming SMS messages. As an example, *Zsone* listens to this *SMS_RECEIVED* event and intercepts or removes all SMS message from particular originating numbers such as "10086" and "10010". The *RogueSPPush* listens to this event to automatically hide and reply to incoming premium-rate service subscription SMS message. In fact, the malware can even discard this *SMS_RECEIVED* event and stop it from further spreading in the system by calling *abortBroadcast()* function. As a result, other apps (including system SMS messaging app) do not even know the arrival of this new SMS message.

During our analysis, we also find that certain malware registers for a variety of events. For example, *AnserverBot* registers for callbacks from 10 different events while *BaseBridge* is interested in 9 different events. The registration of a large number of events is expected to allow the malware to reliably or quickly launch the carried payloads.

In addition, we also observe some malware samples directly hijack the entry activity of the host apps, which will be triggered when the user clicks the app icon on the home screen or an intent with action *ACTION_MAIN* is received by the app. The hijacking of the entry activity allows the malware to immediately bootstrap its service before starting the host app's primary activity. For example, *DroidDream* replaces the original entry activity with its own *com.android.root.main* so that it can gain control even before the original activity *com.codingcaveman.SoloTrial.SplashActivity* is launched. Some malware may also hijack certain UI interaction events (e.g., button clicking). An example is the *Zsone* malware that invokes its own SMS sending code inside the *onClick()* function of the host app.

2.2.3 Malicious Payloads

As existing Android malware can be largely characterized by their carried payloads, we also survey our dataset and partition the payload functionalities into four different categories: *privilege escalation*, *remote control*, *financial charges*, and *personal information stealing*.

2.2.3.1 Privilege Escalation

The Android platform is a complicated system that consists of not only the Linux kernel, but also the entire Android framework with more than 90 open-source libraries,

Table 2.3 The list of platform-level root exploits and their uses in existing Android malware

Vulnerable program	Root exploit	Release date	Malware with the exploit
Linux kernel	Asroot [7]	2009/08/16	Asroot
init (<= 2.2)	Exploid [5]	2010/07/15	DroidDream, zHash, DroidKungFu[1235]
adbd (<= 2.2.1)	RATC [9]	2010/08/21	DroidDream, BaseBridge
zygote (<= 2.2.1)	Zimperlich [38]	2011/02/24	DroidKungFu [1235], DroidDeluxe DroidCoupon
ashmem (<= 2.2.1)	KillingInThe NameOf [3]	2011/01/06	–
vold (<= 2.3.3)	GingerBreak [36]	2011/04/21	GingerMaster
libsysutils (<= 2.3.6)	zergRush [26]	2011/10/10	–

including WebKit, SQLite, and OpenSSL. The complexity naturally introduces software vulnerabilities that can be potentially exploited for privilege escalation. In Table 2.3, we show the list of known Android platform-level vulnerabilities that can be exploited for privilege exploitations. Inside the table, we also show the list of Android malware that actively exploit these vulnerabilities to facilitate the execution of their payloads.

Overall, there are a small number of platform-level vulnerabilities that are being actively exploited in the wild. The top three exploits are *exploid*, *RATC* (or *RageAgainstTheCage*), and *Zimperlich*. We point out that if the *RATC* exploit is launched within a running app, it is effectively exploiting the bug in the *zygote* daemon, *not* the intended *adbd* daemon, thus behavoring as the *Zimperlich* exploit. Considering the similar nature of these two vulnerabilities, we use *RATC* to represent both of them.

From our analysis, one alarming result is that among 1260 samples in our dataset, 463 of them (36.7 %) embed at least one root exploit (Table 2.4). In terms of the popularity of each individual exploit, there are 389, 440, 4, and 8 samples that contain *exploid*, *RATC*, *GingerBreak*, and *Asroot*, respectively. Also, it is not uncommon for a malware to have two or more root exploits to maximize its chances for successful exploitations on multiple platform versions. (In our dataset, there are 378 samples with more than one root exploit.)

2.2.3.2 Remote Control

During our analysis to examine the remote control functionality among the malware payloads, we are surprised to note that 1172 samples (93.0 %) communicate with remote servers or turn the infected phones into bots for remote control. Specifically, there are 1171 samples that use the HTTP-based web traffic to communicate with remote servers and receive bot commands from their C&C servers.

Table 2.4 An overview of existing Android malware (Part II: malicious payloads)

	Privilege escalation				Remote control		Financial charges			Personal information stealing		
	Exploid	RATC	Ginger break	Asroot	NET	SMS	Phone call	SMS	Block SMS	SMS	Phone number	User account
ADRD					✓							
AnserverBot					✓			✓†				
Asroot				✓								
BaseBridge		✓			✓		✓	✓†	✓			
BeanBot					✓		✓	✓†	✓		✓	
BgServ					✓			✓†	✓		✓	
CoinPirate					✓			✓†	✓	✓		
Crusewin					✓			✓	✓	✓		
DogWars					✓			✓				
DroidCoupon		✓			✓							
DroidDeluxe		✓										
DroidDream	✓	✓			✓							
DroidDreamLight					✓							✓
DroidKungFu1	✓	✓			✓						✓	
DroidKungFu2	✓	✓			✓						✓	
DroidKungFu3	✓	✓			✓						✓	
DroidKungFu4					✓							
DroidKungFu5	✓				✓						✓	
DroidKungFuUpdate		✓										
Endofday					✓			✓			✓	
FakeNetflix												✓
FakePlayer								✓‡				
GamblerSMS								✓†		✓		
Geinimi					✓			✓†		✓	✓	

(Continued)

Table 2.4 (Continued)

	Privilege escalation				Remote control		Financial charges			Personal information stealing		
	Exploid	RATC	Ginger break	Asroot	NET	SMS	Phone call	SMS	Block SMS	SMS	Phone number	User account
GGTracker								√‡	√	√	√	
GingerMaster			√		√					√	√	
GoldDream					√		√	√†		√	√	
Gone60										√	√	
GPSSMSSpy												
HippoSMS								√‡	√			
Jifake								√‡				
jSMSHider					√			√†	√			
KMin					√			√†	√			
Lovetrap								√†	√			
NickyBot						√				√		
Nickyspy					√					√		
Pjapps					√			√†	√	√	√	
Plankton					√							
RogueLemon					√			√†	√	√		
RogueSPPush								√‡	√			
SMSReplicator										√		
SndApps					√							√
Spitmo								√†	√	√	√	
TapSnake					√							
Walkinwat					√			√‡		√		
YZHC								√†	√	√	√	
zHash	√											
Zitmo										√		
Zsone								√‡	√			

We also observe that some malware families attempt to be stealthy by encrypting the URLs of remote C&C servers as well as their communication with C&C servers. For example, *Pjapps* develops its own encoding scheme to encrypt the C&C server addresses. One of its samples encodes its C&C server *mobilemeego91.com* into *2maodb3ialke8mdeme3gkos9g1icaofm*. *DroidKungFu3* employs the standard AES encryption scheme and uses the key *Fuck_sExy-aLl!Pw* to hide its C&C servers. *Geinimi* similarly applies DES encryption scheme (with the key *0x01020304050607-08*) to encrypt its communication to the remote C&C server.

During our study, we also find that most C&C servers are registered in domains controlled by attackers themselves. However, we also identify cases where the C&C servers are hosted in public clouds. For instance, the *Plankton* spyware dynamically fetches and runs its payload from a server hosted in the Amazon cloud. Most recently, attackers are even turning to public blog servers as their C&C servers. *AnserverBot* is one example that uses two popular public blog services, i.e., *Sina* and *Baidu*, as its C&C servers to retrieve the latest payloads and new C&C URLs (Chap. 3).

2.2.3.3 Financial Charge

Beside privilege escalation and remote control, we also look into the motivations behind malware infection. In particular, we study whether malware will intentionally cause financial charges to infected users.

One profitable way for attackers is to surreptitiously subscribe to (attacker-controlled) premium-rate services, such as by sending SMS messages. On Android, there is a permission-guarded function *sendTextMessage* that allows for sending an SMS message in the background without user's awareness. We are able to confirm this type of attacks targeting users in Russia, United States, and China. The very first Android malware *FakePlayer* sends SMS message "798657" to multiple premium-rate numbers in Russia. *GGTracker* automatically signs up the infected user to premium services in US without user's knowledge. *Zsone* sends SMS messages to premium-rate numbers in China without user's consent. In total, there are 55 samples (4.4 %) falling in 7 different families (tagged with ‡ in Table 2.4) that send SMS messages to the premium-rate numbers hardcoded in the infected apps.

Moreover, some malware choose *not* to hard-code premium-rate numbers. Instead, they leverage the flexible remote control to push down the numbers at runtime. In our dataset, there are 13 such malware families (tagged with † in Table 2.4). Apparently, these malware families are stealthier than earlier ones because the destination number will not be known by simply analyzing the infected apps.

In our analysis, we also observe that by automatically subscribing to premium-rate services, these malware families need to reply to certain SMS messages. This may due to the second-confirmation policy required in some countries such as China. Specifically, to sign up a premium-rate service, the user must reply to a confirming SMS message sent from the service provider to finalize or activate the service subscription. To avoid users from being notified, they will take care of replying to these confirming messages by themselves. As an example, *RogueSPPush* will automatically reply "Y" to such incoming messages in the background; *GGTracker* will reply "YES" to one premium number, 99735, to activate the subscribed service. Similarly, to prevent users from knowing subsequent billing-related messages, they choose to filter these SMS messages as well. This behavior is present in a number of malware, including *Zsone*, *RogueSPPush*, and *GGTracker*.

Besides these premium-rate numbers, some malware also leverage the same functionality by sending SMS messages to other phone numbers. Though less serious than previous ones, they still result in certain financial charges especially when the user does not have an unlimited messaging plan. For example, *DogWars* sends SMS messages to all the contacts in the phone without user's awareness. Other malware may also make background phone calls. With the same remote control capability, the destination number can be provided from a remote C&C server, as shown in *Geinimi*.

2.2.3.4 Information Collection

In addition to the above payloads, we also find that malware are actively harvesting various information on the infected phones, including SMS messages, phone numbers as well as user accounts. In particular, there are 13 malware families (138 samples) in our dataset that collect SMS messages, 15 families (563 samples) gather phone numbers, and 3 families (43 samples) obtain and upload the information about user accounts. For example, *SndApps* collects users' email addresses and sends them to a remote server. *FakeNetflix* gathers users' Netflix accounts and passwords by providing a fake but seeming identical Netflix UI.

We consider the collection of users' SMS messages is a highly suspicious behavior. The user credential may be included in SMS messages. For example, both *Zitmo* (the *Zeus* version on Android) and *Spitmo* (the *SpyEpy* version on Android) attempt to intercept SMS verification messages and then upload them to a remote server. If successful, the attacker may use them to generate fraudulent transactions on behalf of infected users.

2.2.4 Permission Usage

For Android apps without root exploits, their capabilities are strictly constrained by the permissions users grant to them. Therefore, it will be interesting to compare top permissions requested by these malicious apps in the dataset with top permissions requested by benign ones. To this end, we have randomly chosen 1260 top free apps downloaded from the official Android Market in the first week of October, 2011. The results are shown in Fig. 2.4.

Based on the comparison, Android permissions such as *INTERNET, READ_ PHONE_STATE, ACCESS_NETWORK_STATE*, and *WRITE_EXTERNAL_STO- RAGE* are widely requested in both malicious and benign apps. The first two are typically needed to allow for the embedded ad libraries to function properly.

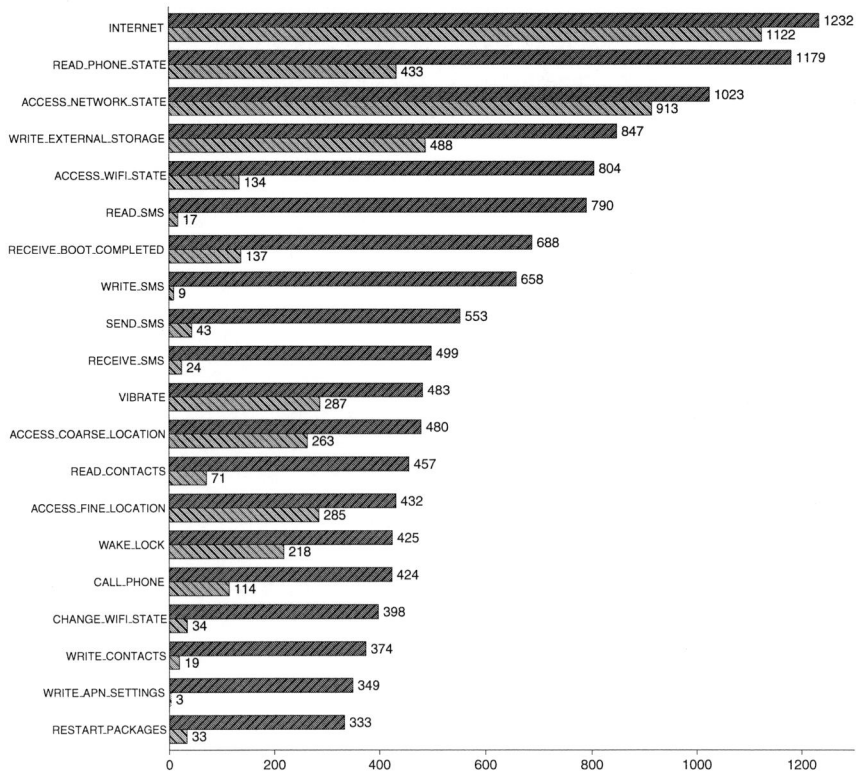

Fig. 2.4 The comparison of top 20 requested permissions by malicious apps (the ▨▨▨ *bar*) and benign apps (the ▧▧▧ *bar*)

But malicious apps clearly tend to request more frequently on the SMS-related permissions, such as *READ_SMS*, *WRITE_SMS*, *RECEIVE_SMS*, and *SEND_SMS*. Specifically, there are 790 samples (62.7 %) in our dataset that request the *READ_SMS* permission, while 17 benign apps (or 1.3 %) request this permission. These results are consistent with the fact that 28 malware families in our dataset (or 45.3 % of the samples) that have the SMS-related malicious functionality.

Also, we observe 688 malware samples request the *RECEIVE_BOOT_COMPLE-TED* permission. This number is five times of that in benign apps (137 samples). This could be due to the fact that malware is more likely to run background services without user's intervention. Note that there are 398 malware samples requesting *CHANGE_WIFI_STATE* permission, which is an order of magnitude higher than that in benign apps (34 samples). That is mainly because the *Exploid* root exploit requires certain hot plug events such as changing the WIFI state, which is related to this permission.

Finally, we notice that malicious apps tend to request more permissions than benign ones. In our dataset, the average number of permissions requested by malicious apps is 11 while the average number requested by benign apps is 4. Among the top 20 permissions, 9 of them are requested by malicious apps on average while 3 of them on average are requested by benign apps.

Chapter 3
Case Studies

In this chapter, we examine three representative Android malware families, i.e., *Plankton*, *DroidKungFu*, and *AnserverBot*, and present a detailed analysis of them.

3.1 Malware I: Plankton

We discovered the *Plankton* spyware in early June, 2011. Different from other Android malware,the *Plankton* spyware does not directly embed its malicious payload in itself. Instead it downloads the payload from a remote server at runtime and then leverages the dynamic loading capability of Dalvik Virtual Machine (or DVM) to dynamically load the payload for execution. *Plankton* is considered the first Android malware in the wild that exploits such dynamic class loading capability to stay stealthy (and dynamically extend its own functionality). At the time when it was discovered, we found more than ten instances of infected apps from different developers on the official Android Market maintained by Google. Our further investigation shows that *Plankton* is mainly developed for the purpose of mobile advertisement. However it obviously crosses the line of being an advertisement library by stealthily and aggressively collecting user's personal data and further employing bot-like capability to execute commands retrieved from remote servers. The discovery of *Plankton* also reveals the uneasy security and privacy threats of aggressive (mobile) advertisement services. In the following, we illustrate how it works and highlight various interesting aspects discovered in our examination.

3.1.1 Phoning Home

The *Plankton* spyware is included in a variety of host apps as a new background service. This background service, even removed from any host app, does not affect in any way the functionality of the host app. This service is invoked

```
POST /ProtocolGW/installation HTTP/1.1
Content-Length: 1242
Content-Type: application/x-www-form-urlencoded
Host: www.searchwebmobile.com
Connection: Keep-Alive

action=get&applicationId=123456789&developerId=987654321&deviceId=354957034053382&currentVersion=-1
&permissions=android.permission.INTERNET%3Bandroid.permission.ACCESS_WIFI_STATE%3Bcom.android.brows
er.permission.WRITE_HISTORY_BOOKMARKS%3Bcom.android.browser.permission.READ_HISTORY_BOOKMARKS%3Bcom
.android.launcher.permission.INSTALL_SHORTCUT%3Bcom.android.launcher.permission.UNINSTALL_SHORTCUT%
3Bcom.android.launcher.permission.READ_SETTINGS%3Bcom.android.launcher.permission.WRITE_SETTINGS%3B
com.htc.launcher.permission.READ_SETTINGS%3Bcom.motorola.launcher.permission.READ_SETTINGS%3Bcom.mo
torola.launcher.permission.WRITE_SETTINGS%3Bcom.motorola.launcher.permission.INSTALL_SHORTCUT%3Bcom
.motorola.launcher.permission.UNINSTALL_SHORTCUT%3Bcom.motorola.dlauncher.permission.READ_SETTINGS%
3Bcom.motorola.dlauncher.permission.WRITE_SETTINGS%3Bcom.motorola.dlauncher.permission.INSTALL_SHOR
TCUT%3Bcom.motorola.dlauncher.permission.UNINSTALL_SHORTCUT%3Bcom.lge.launcher.permission.READ_SETT
INGS%3Bcom.lge.launcher.permission.WRITE_SETTINGS%3Bcom.lge.launcher.permission.INSTALL_SHORTCUT%3B
com.lge.launcher.permission.UNINSTALL_SHORTCUT%3Bandroid.permission.READ_CONTACTS%3Bandroid.permiss
ion.READ_PHONE_STATE%3Bandroid.permission.READ_LOGS%3B

HTTP/1.1 200 OK
Date: Sun, 05 Jun 2011 04:30:33 GMT
Server: Apache-Coyote/1.1
Content-Length: 76
Connection: keep-alive

url=http://www.searchwebmobile.com/ProtocolGW/;fileName=plankton_v0.0.4.jar;
```

Fig. 3.1 The captured HTTP POST message sent by *Plankton*

in the modified *onCreate()* method of the main activity inside the app. In other words, when the infected app runs, it will immediately bring up the background service. Then the background service will start to collect information, including the device ID as well as the list of granted permissions to the infected app, and send them back to a remote server through an HTTP POST message.

In Fig. 3.1, we show the captured HTTP POST message sent by *Plankton* to its remote server. The message contains different types of information, including the application identity (or applicationID), the version number, the current action being taken, as well as the identify of the phone (i.e., IMEI number) and the list of permissions requested by this current app. Note that sending the list of permissions required by the app to the remote server is considered suspicious because the remote server may now use this list to customize the payloads downloaded to the client for targeted execution. Figure 3.1 also shows the corresponding HTTP response message from the *Plankton* server.

3.1.2 Dynamic Execution

After receiving a specific request from a client, the *Plankton* server will push its payload (in the form of a JAR file) back to the client. This payload contains the code which can be dynamically loaded and executed by *Plankton* at runtime. Specifically, *Plankton* leverages the dynamic class loading capability to load the downloaded payload into memory and then invoke the code (via the Java reflection). By doing so, *Plankton* becomes stealthy by making the runtime code unknown in advance. As a result, it has the potential of completely bypassing static analysis employed

```
public enum Commands
{
    ...
    static
    {
        ACTIVATION      = new Commands("ACTIVATION", 1, "Activation", "/activate");
        HOMEPAGE        = new Commands("HOMEPAGE", 2, "Homepage", "/homepage");
        COMMANDS_STATUS = new Commands("COMMANDS_STATUS", 3, "CommandsStatus", "/commandstatus");
        BOOKMARKS       = new Commands("BOOKMARKS", 4, "Bookmarks", "/bookmarks");
        SHORTCUTS       = new Commands("SHORTCUTS", 5, "Shortcuts", "/shortcuts");
        HISTORY         = new Commands("HISTORY", 6, "History", "/history");
        TERMINATE       = new Commands("TERMINATE", 7, "Terminate", "/terminate");
        STATUS          = new Commands("STATUS", 8, "Status", "/status");
        DUMP_LOG        = new Commands("DUMP_LOG", 9, "DumpLog", "/dumplog");
        UNEXP_EXCEPTION = new Commands("UNEXP_EXCEPTION", 10, "UnexpectedException", "/unexpectedexception");
        UPGRADE         = new Commands("UPGRADE", 11, "Upgrade", "/installation");
        INSTALLATION    = new Commands("INSTALLATION", 12, "Installation", "/installation");
    }
}
```

Fig. 3.2 The list of commands supported in *Plankton*

by most anti-virus engines. Such design also reflects an earlier research prototype named *RootStrap* [25] that uses similar design to download and execute root exploits at runtime.

During our investigation, we have successfully downloaded the *Plankton* payload with two different versions: *plankton_v0.0.3.jar* and *plankton_v0.0.4.jar*. Our analysis shows that while they do not contain root exploits, they support a number of bot-related commands that can be remotely invoked. In Fig. 3.2, we show the list of commands supported in version 0.0.4. In essence, the */bookmarks* command collects the bookmark information on the phone; */shortcuts* allows for the installation or removal of home screen shortcuts; */history* steals browser history information; and */dumplog* essentially executes the *logcat* command to collect runtime log information. Earlier reports show that highly sensitive private information may exist as plain text in the runtime log. We also identified an interesting function that if invoked can be used to collect user's accounts. Though this function is not linked to any supported command, its presence as well as the capability of dynamically loading a new payload can readily turn stealing user's accounts or even launching root exploits into reality.

3.2 Malware II: DroidKungFu

In the same month of June 2011, we also came across another Android malware named *DroidKungFu*. This is a sophisticated malware by employing several techniques that were not common in other Android malware at that time. After the initial discovery, we also detected two variants (*DroidKungFu2* and *DroidKungFu3*) in July and August, respectively. These two variants evolve further to embed native payloads and encrypted C&C servers to evade possible detection. Two months later, the fourth variant (*DroidKungFu4*) was detected with both encrypted native payloads and C&C servers. In the meantime, there is another variant called *DroidKungFuUpdate* [10] that utilizes the update attack to download an "updated" version, which is actually a malware. Also in the same time frame, we detected another variant called

DroidKungFuSapp. The flurry of new *DroidKungFu* variants clearly indicates the rapid evolution of Android malware in the wild. In Table 3.1, we summarize these six *DroidKungFu* variants. Next, we will zoom into these *DroidKungFu* variants and illustrate various aspects of them.

3.2.1 Root Exploits

By employing root exploits, Android malware can potentially obtain root privilege and bypass any built-in security mechanism in Android (e.g., without being constrained by Android permissions). Among the six variants we analyzed, we found four of them actually contain root exploits.

However different from others that also embed root exploits, *DroidKungFu* encrypts the actual root exploits and disguises them as local resource files under *assets* directory (that by convention is typically used to store assets files, not the code). To the best of our knowledge, it is the first time for an Android malware to include encrypted root exploits. To further increase the chance of successfully "rooting" the system, *DroidKungFu* uses two different root exploits and can switch to another one if the first try is failed.

The use of encryption is helpful for *DroidKungFu* to evade detection. And different variants tend to use different encryption keys to better protect themselves. For example, the key used in *DroidKungFu1* is *Fuck_sExy-aLl!Pw*, which has been changed to *Stak_yExy-eLt!Pw* in *DroidKungFu4*.

It is interesting to notice that in *DroidKungFu1*, the file name with the encrypted root exploit is "ratc"—the acronym of *RageAgainstTheCage*. In *DroidKungFu2* and *DroidKungFu3*, this file name with the same root exploit has been changed to "*myicon*", pretending to be an icon file.

3.2.2 Command and Control (C&C) Servers

All *DroidKungFu* variants communicate with remote C&C servers to receive and execute the corresponding commands. To hide the existence (and the addresses) of C&C servers, the malware continuously changes the way to store theses addresses. For instance, in *DroidKungFu1*, the address of C&C server is saved in plain-text in a Java class file, which can be easily retrieved by disassembling the class. In *DroidKungFu2*, this C&C server address is in plain-text but has been moved to a native program, which is harder to understand than Java class file. Also the number of C&C servers increases from 1 to 3 to make the connection to remote server more reliable. In *DroidKungFu3*, similar with *DroidKungFu1*, the address is in Java class. However this address is encrypted and cannot be obtained directly. In *DroidKungFu4*, it moves the C&C address back to a native program as *DroidKungFu2* but in cipertext. In *DroidKungFuSapp*, it uses a totally new C&C server and a different home-made encryption scheme.

Table 3.1 The overview of six *DroidKungFu* malware variants

	Root exploits			C&C			Number	Malicious component	Embedded Apk
	Exploid	RATC	Encrypted	In native	In Java	Encrypted			
DroidKungFu1	✓	✓	✓		✓		1	com.google.ssearch	plaintext
DroidKungFu2	✓	✓	✓	✓			3	com.eguan.state	none
DroidKungFu3	✓	✓	✓	✓	✓	✓	3	com.google.update	encrypted
DroidKungFu4				✓	✓	✓	3	com.safesys	none
DroidKungFuSapp	✓	✓	✓		✓		1	com.mjdc.sapp	none
DroidKungFuUpdate	–	–	–	–	–	–	–	–	none

3.2.3 Payloads

DroidKungFu variants are typically distributed in form of repackaged apps. They infect the host apps by injecting malicious payloads, either in Dalvik bytecode or native binary code, into these host apps. In addition, they also embed a child app that contains almost identical functionality to the malicious payload injected to the repackaged app. This embedded app can be installed silently without user's awareness once the malware successfully obtains the root privilege. As a result, the installation of this embedded app will ensure that even the repackaged app has been removed, it can continue to be functional. Moreover, in *DroidKungFu1*, the embedded app will show a fake Google Search icon while in *DroidKungFu2*, the embedded app is encrypted and will not display any icon on the infected phone.

3.2.4 Obfuscation, JNI, and Others

To prevent it from being analyzed, *DroidKungFu* also aggressively employs various obfuscation techniques. For example, it not only encrypts constant strings in its payloads, but also heavily makes use of encryption to hide the existence of root exploits and C&C servers. Moreover it aggressively obfuscates the class name in the malicious payload, and exploits JNI interfaces to increase the difficulty for analysis and detection. For instance, both *DroidKungFu2* and *DroidKungFu4* use a native program (through JNI) to communicate with and fetch bot commands from remote servers.

The *DroidKungFuUpdate* variant takes a more stealthy approach by using the update attack (Chap. 2) to launch its payloads. With its stealthiness, it managed into the official Android Market for users to download, reflecting the evolution trend of Android malware to be more stealthy in their design and infection. More specifically, it embeds its own (obfuscated) malicious code in a host app. When this ("clean") host app is uploaded to Android Market, it does not exhibit any security problem. However, when this app is downloaded to run on a user's phone, it will display a pop-up window to ask user to update the app (Fig. 3.3a). If the user chooses to update it, it will immediately download another app from a remote server (Fig. 3.3b). It turns out that the downloaded app is not the updated version, but the *DroidKungFu4* malware.

3.3 Malware III: AnserverBot

Next, we examine the third representative Android malware named *AnserverBot*, which we discovered in September 2011. This malware piggybacks on legitimate apps and is being actively distributed among a few third-party Android market-places. In terms of sophistication, the malware is comparable to earlier *DroidKungFu*

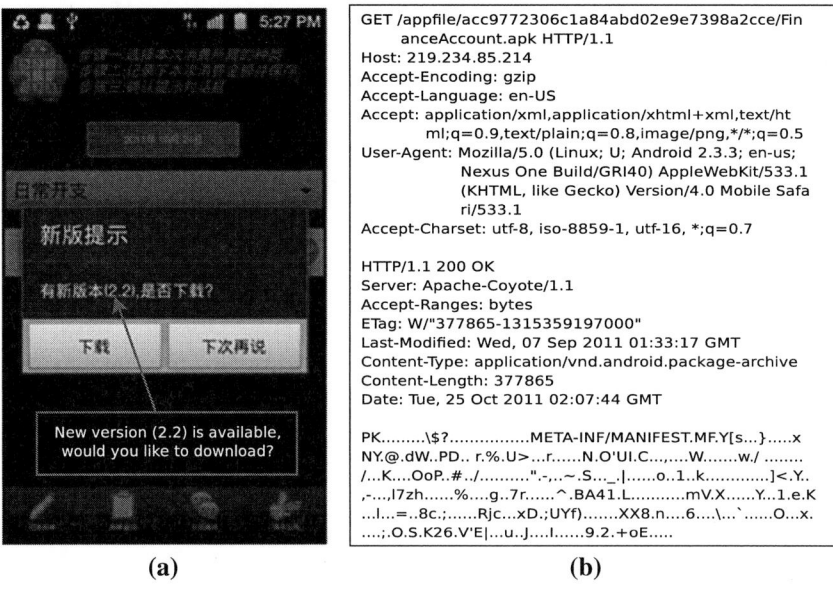

(a)   **(b)**

Fig. 3.3 An update attack from *DroidKungFuUpdate*. **a** The update dialog. **b** The HTTP traffic (for malware downloading)

malware by aggressively exploiting several advanced techniques to evade detection and analysis, which have not been seen before. After more than one-week in-depth investigation [4], we believe this malware evolves from earlier *BaseBridge* malware [11]. In the following, we will highlight key techniques employed by *AnserverBot*.

3.3.1 Anti-Analysis

Though *AnserverBot* itself repackages legitimate apps for infection, it is designed to detect whether it has been tampered with or not. Specifically, when it runs, it will check the signature or the integrity of the current (repackaged) app before unfolding its payloads. This mechanism is in place to thwart possible reverse engineering efforts.

Moreover, *AnserverBot* aggressively obfuscates its internal classes, methods, and fields to make them humanly unreadable. Also, it intentionally partitions the main payload into three related apps: one is the host app and the other two are embedded apps. The two embedded apps share the same name *com.sec.android.touchScreen. server* but with different functionality. One such app will be installed through the update attack while the other will be dynamically loaded without being actually installed (similar to *Plankton*). The functionality partitioning and coordination, as well as aggressive obfuscation, make its analysis very challenging.

We have the reason to believe that *AnserverBot* is inspired by the dynamic loading mechanism from *Plankton*. In particular, the dynamic mechanisms to retrieve and load remote code is not available in earlier *BaseBridge* malware. In other words, it exploits the class loading feature in Dalvik virtual machine to load and execute the malicious payload at run time. By employing this dynamic loading behavior, *AnserverBot* can greatly protect itself from being detected by existing anti-virus software. Moreover, with such dynamic capability in place, malware authors can instantly upgrade the payloads while still taking advantage of current infection base.

Another related self-protection feature used in *AnserverBot* is that it can detect the presence of certain mobile anti-virus software. If any of them is detected, *AnserverBot* will attempt to stop it and further display a dialog window, informing the user that the particular app is stopped unexpectedly.

3.3.2 Command and Control (C&C) Servers

One interesting aspect of *AnserverBot* is its C&C servers. In particular, it supports two types of C&C servers. The first one is similar to traditional C&C servers from which to receive the command. The second one instead is used to upgrade its payload and/or the new address of the first type C&C server. Surprisingly, the second type is based on (encrypted) blog contents, which are maintained by popular blog service providers. In other words, *AnserverBot* connects to the public blog site to fetch the (encrypted) current C&C server and the new (encrypted) payload. This functionality can ensure that even if the first type C&C server is offline, the new C&C server can still be pushed to the malware through this public blog. As an example, the content of a particular blog entry is "*v____:HoiprJbh9CVN9wnQ0w7O84FePwnYPJShHIEO7x0pHxMO*", which turns out to be an encrypted address "http://b3.8866.org:8080/jk.action". This is rather interesting as it is the first Android malware that exploits public blogs as its C&C servers to deliver various payloads.

AnserverBot can also dynamically upgrade itself when a new version is available. Specifically, if there is a new version, the C&C server, when contacted, will respond back with the latest version number as well as the related download URL. After receiving the response, *AnserverBot* will notice the newer version and then decide whether to download it. If yes, it will fetch the newer version from the download URL specified in the response. During our investigation, we have identified more than 20 different versions of payloads posted in this blog. Six of them were posted within one single week, which clearly shows its rapid evolution in the wild. In Fig. 3.4, we show the captured network traffic when *AnserverBot* downloads a newer version, which was stored in the same public blog website as shown in Fig. 3.5.

Our investigation also shows that the *AnserverBot* payload is actually a recent variant of *BaseBridge*, which was first discovered in May 2011. The *BaseBridge* malware has been known to receive premium numbers from remote C&C servers and then send out SMS text messages to them.

```
00000000    48 54 54 50 2f 31 2e 31    20 32 30 30 20 4f 4b 0d    HTTP/1.1  200 OK.
00000010    0a 53 65 72 76 65 72 3a    20 6e 67 69 6e 78 2f 30    .Server:  nginx/0
00000020    2e 37 2e 36 32 0d 0a 44    61 74 65 3a 20 57 65 64    .7.62..D ate: Wed
00000030    2c 20 32 31 20 53 65 70    20 32 30 31 31 20 30 31    , 21 Sep  2011 01
00000040    3a 34 34 3a 31 36 20 47    4d 54 0d 0a 43 6f 6e 74    :44:16 G MT..Cont
00000050    65 6e 74 2d 54 79 70 65    3a 20 74 65 78 74 2f 68    ent-Type : text/h
00000060    74 6d 6c 0d 0a 43 6f 6e    6e 65 63 74 69 6f 6e 3a    tml..Con nection:
00000070    20 6b 65 65 70 2d 61 6c    69 76 65 0d 0a 56 61 72    keep-al ive..Var
00000080    79 3a 20 41 63 63 65 70    74 2d 45 6e 63 6f 64 69    y: Accep t-Encodi
...
00005380    09 09 09 76 5f 5f 5f 5f    5f 3a 79 6a 45 4a 54 54    ...v____ _:yjEJTT
00005390    6c 53 76 53 53 56 53 47    52 70 39 4e 41 53 53 53    lSvSSVSG Rp9NASSS
000053A0    53 53 3c 77 62 72 3e 53    53 53 53 53 53 53 53 53    SS<wbr>S SSSSSSSS
000053B0    53 53 6b 53 53 53 53 37    57 42 35 72 74 68 79 3c    SSkSSSS7 WB5rthy<
000053C0    77 62 72 3e 4f 56 33 4a    65 4a 34 71 39 36 73 53    wbr>OV3J eJ4q96sS
000053D0    72 63 35 4f 73 37 67 36    57 73 7a 38 3c 77 62 72    rc5Os7g6 Wsz8<wbr
000053E0    3e 68 4a 6e 39 39 50 36    4f 36 55 61 52 67 6b 53    >hJn99P6 O6UaRgkS
000053F0    5a 73 75 34 75 34 78 74    4b 3c 77 62 72 3e 79 67    Zsu4u4xt K<wbr>yg
00005400    32 35 4f 50 45 57 73 75    70 47 68 7a 2f 34 2f 72    25OPEWsu pGhz/4/r
```

Fig. 3.4 The captured HTTP response when a new version is being downloaded

```
v_____:yjEJTTlSvSSVSGRp9NASSSSSSSSSSSSSSSSSSSkSSSS7WB5rthyOV3JeJ4q96sSrc5Os7g6Ws
z8hJn99P6O6UaRgkSZsu4u4xtKyg25OPEWsupGhz/4/r6NeP+AdAJFRyDIDCcc+rLrL2Hm9V/Yv5+
SAh9fOeZVhVjBTRQJSSSMPSSS/a3xRkVq7B03+EW5ZZ7D+LjZmfHO+kk/OjE1MTpnHkplMiWUywrP
wBY7QCyDE3fQw9wqCBYAa3jPKLoG/3CQ72UBxPMBase4L/2Gply3Rz9DgXTg+J6OeuwrqksdKwMj2
nM3IH89zUIaU0CUsxZKMXbNEHzPgIAZHNa27z8oQJji2Y7bPJI1qh3qWfM+L49oJv8bUC8y2w/bZS
i2n92hKdY+sLynu6rzcUEWd1xD99zw0002P5Dg+AjuBzhfPlMap2NeXeNZFedf1qJbmdZrMvDsIqD
b/2u0mDE9Qztt3qRVHg/15gX/3zV01hTV6ilH4Ym/Z3GaCHiPcLCSqZBRRyCQcKJQmGONIYgBBGjN
emVAfEU/YaGAoATBhmtRje2iqh+dYfR92rI+X/XPIs4ApKBjpqoDoHJ4gP4mHhSI7KuzAqrNzSH3o
LM3QbOqvO952ruguGjd9RsLjQheJLEXSDkT7owFe5W2g64haimNxKqHvTqvx/+EQqgqwAkLJisJFc
el01Nyyo/zx6rqJDcITor8R3aFLzoR2A86FbW7NMWCAzWnbPSGP76Y9xwx7pejz7zj295WDtswj53
...
2heRNnK/nLdbgVrjhqEeTBWl/4Mbg6GXq9K9112UpjaQMUE/bcDXu1vBgINrNgjSLUufId2O1L/QR
PpZMVFPBGx9dn9OdWRd/q4/915/6T1jMBM8cKJQ/2708tB/e22yAJVGrxwajAcMuYjDx0uHa42tGr
dP06QXLFd7qQEgZruOR3uQ2wahcLUikVV7aM1nLA9VjddtJK9pSe6QuqsP+PQvoOsyK2jJhfn1Viw
SsPaqaH3mJH664/4+gASbgFPCqMvGObu+K+sIus1ejfL7iGMk0Ut+ZhOME0FvV1iLBzVYjUJrEE7N
umZZ6qe1q15E/K9iiSUKdXDI7GcsvO6GBhAwcqMz0zb0JzqXS3MSpkmKZOj9UB5g56AxvxR2QT0Yc
eLPsbudYyjve6pCWuJg1i9pI+r/oNqDG1DNqJFAK1HOGD57/eu+Wlv65PBqXhOmd47VhIjA2AKLhA
pORcid/o2/3//GzqUd+F/WawaFAf/pBe+J7jK/4gxpNAz/5DsMt/yh/YhnyG/bEJQa6ARYaJ+TQyj
CR//GcdIepm+Hrd+86No/R/0Cd+1Q4/HChQeESw++bdF6qA//DA/peAweO5/OFPU2ZGMZAqImLDGi
A/NtWdz/thCdYT1cYrV6nkpcORbSSTg8SSSyjETS51SkSSVSSnS+K1hG+QTujwzHSSS8xYSSSySSS
SSSSSSSSSSSSSSSSSSStVO7KTmyjEkTnSSSSSTSSjSfYSSSSs1SSSSSS__
```

Fig. 3.5 The content of a particular public blog entry (to update *AnserverBot* itself)

All in all, the combination of *Plankton*-style stealthy dynamic code loading and execution with various code/data obfuscation techniques eventually leads to the emergence of the sophisticated *AnserverBot* malware.

Chapter 4
Discussion

Our study of existing Android malware, including an in-depth examination of representative ones, has clearly shown that they pose a serious threat we are facing today. To make matters worse, with limited resources and battery, commodity mobile devices also pose a stringent runtime environment that is different from our desktop PCs. Such difference could preclude the deployment of sophisticated detection techniques that are developed for desktop PCs. From another perspective, the presence of centralized marketplaces in current mobile ecosystems does provide unique advantages in blocking mobile malware from entering the marketplaces in the first place. In the following, we draw several insights from our characterization to mitigate or defend against mobile malware in general.

First, our characterization shows that most existing Android malware (86.0 %) repackage other legitimate (popular) apps, which indicates that we might be able to effectively mitigate the threat by policing existing marketplaces for repackaging detection. However, the challenges lie in the large volume of new apps uploaded on a daily basis as well as the accuracy needed for repackaging detection. In addition, the popularity of alternative marketplaces will also add significant challenges. Though there is no clear solution in sight, we do argue for a joint effort involving all parties in the ecosystem to spot and discourage repackaged apps.

Second, our characterization also indicates that more than one third (36.7 %) of Android malware enclose platform-level exploits to escalate their privilege. Unfortunately, the open Android platform has the well-known "fragmentation" problem, which leads to a long vulnerable time window of current mobile devices before a patch can be actually deployed. Worse, the current platform still lacks many desirable security features. ASLR was not added until very recently in Android 4.0. Other security features such as TrustZone and XN (eXecute-Never) need to be gradually rolled out to raise the bar for exploitation. Moreover, our analysis reveals that the dynamic loading ability of both native code and Dalvik code are being actively abused by existing malware (e.g., *DroidKungFu* and *AnserverBot*). There is a need to develop effective solutions to prevent them from being abused while still allowing legitimate uses to proceed.

Third, our characterization shows that existing malware (45.3 %) tend to subscribe to premium-rate services with background SMS messages. Related to that, most existing malware intercept incoming SMS messages (e.g., to block billing information or sidestep the second-confirmation requirement). This problem might be rooted in the lack of fine-grain control of related APIs (e.g., *sendTextMessage*). Specifically, the coarse-grained Android permission model can be possibly expanded to include additional context information to better facilitate users to make sound and informed decisions.

Last but not least, during the process of collecting malware samples into our current dataset, we felt the strong community need to unify our knowledge and collectively elevate our defense capability, which does call for necessary cooperation and innovation from academia, industry, and research labs. Such need also drives our recent launch of the *Android Malware Genome Project*.

Chapter 5
Additional Reading

In this book, while we aim to make it accessible to those new to the area, we do not intend to provide a comprehensive tutorial on various aspects of Android malware. In the following, we provide relevant references and additional readings for interested readers who want to have a broader understanding of this field.

5.1 Books

5.1.1 Malware Detection and Defense

Published in 2006, Christodorescu et al.'s book [44] covers various aspects in malware research. While it mainly studies PC malware, the fundamental concepts still apply to mobile malware research. Another book [63] from Lee et al. provides various methods to detect and analyze botnet behaviors, which can benefit the research on Android malware as well. Especially, as our dataset shows that more than 90 % of existing Android malware will communicate with remote servers and exhibit bot-like behavior (Chap. 2), the insights gleaned from earlier botnet defense can be equally applied here. As an example, the book (Chap. 7) describes an automatic way to discover trigger behavior in traditional botnets, which can be readily applied to detect Android botnets. Most recently, a new book [74] from Yin et al. proposes an emulator-based system for automatic malware analysis. A similar system can be built for Android malware as well. From another perspective, Masud et al.'s book [64] explores the usage of data mining techniques for malware detection. They could lead to interesting solutions for mitigating and detecting Android malware, especially due to the large number of Android apps available for analysis.

One insight provided by our malware characterization (Chap. 2) is that 86.0 % of existing Android malware are repackaged apps. Hence, how to detect repackaged apps and how to prevent apps from being repackaged become two interesting research problems. Silvio et al.'s book [70] on software similarity can be leveraged to detect repackaged apps by comparing the similarity of different apps. From another perspective, the book [45] from Collberg et al. contains different protection mechanisms for traditional software, which may be potentially used for smartphone app protection.

5.1.2 Smartphone (Apps) Security

Dunham's book [47] is one of the few that specialize on mobile malware attack and defense. It describes the mobile malware history between 2000 and 2008. As expected, they are primarily on the Symbian platform. It also discusses possible protection mechanisms on various mobile platforms such as Symbian, BlackBerry, J2ME, and Windows Mobile. While the targeted malware are likely outdated nowadays, by reading this book, readers can still gain a better knowledge of the history as well as the ongoing arm race between offensive malware and their defense. The managed code rootkit proposed in Metula's book [65] also demonstrates a potential attack to managed runtime environments, which are being used by Android and the latest Windows Phone. To our best knowledge, this attack has not really appeared in the wild yet. However, it does not mean such attack will not show up in the future.

Dwivedi et al.'s book [48] is another great reference especially for developers who want to have a good understanding of various security mechanisms in existing smartphone platforms. The first part examines different smartphone platforms and studies their security features while the second part explores potential attack surfaces, including mobile HTML, bluetooth and SMS, and further suggests possible solutions. The book from Zdziarski [75] also similarly exposes possible attack surfaces related to iOS apps.

From another perspective, Hoog's books [59, 60] primarily focus on mobile forensics on Android and iOS. They provide a relatively comprehensive coverage of both platforms and also include additional security investigation from the forensic perspective. While these two books are not directly related to malware, the analysis methodologies described in these books are applicable for mobile malware analysis.

5.2 Conference and Workshop Proceedings

Smartphone security and privacy has recently become an active topic. There exist a few relevant academic conferences [2, 15, 20, 33] that solicit topics on various aspects of security and privacy on smartphones and mobile devices. In addition, there also exist two new annual academic workshops with an exclusive focus on mobile security and privacy. They are ACM CCS Workshop on Security and Privacy in Smartphones and Mobile Devices (SPSM) [1] (in its second year as of 2012) and Mobile Security Technologies [19] (in its first year as of 2012). In the following, we also summarize most relevant papers in this field.

PiOS [49] and TaintDroid [50] are two recent systems that expose possible privacy leaks of mobile apps on iOS and Android platforms. Comdroid [43, 54] and Woodpecker [56] expose the confused deputy problem [58] on Android, which prompts a series of solutions [42, 46, 54]. Stowaway [52] exposes the overprivilege problem (where an app requests more permissions than it uses) in existing apps. Schrittwieser et al. [68] reports certain security flaws in network-facing messaging apps. Traynor et al. [71] characterizes the impact of mobile botnets on the mobile network. AdRisk [55] systematically identifies potential risks from in-app advertisement libraries.

To improve the smartphone security and privacy, a number of solutions have also been proposed. Specifically, Apex [66], Aurasium [72], AppFence [61], MockDroid [41] and TISSA [79] extend the current Android framework or repackage the apps to provide find-grained access control of system resources from untrusted third-party apps. Saint [67] protects the exposed interfaces of an app to others by allowing the app developers to define related security policies for runtime enforcement. Kirin [51] blocks the installation of suspicious apps by examining the existence of certain dangerous permission combination. L4Android [62] and Cells [40] run multiply OSes on a single smartphone for improved isolation and security. AdSplit [69] separates the app itself from advertisement libraries.

With a focus on mobile malware, Felt et al. [53] surveys 46 samples on three different mobile platforms, i.e., iOS, Android and Symbian, analyzes their incentives, and discusses possible defenses. DroidRanger [78] and RiskRanker [57] detect malicious apps in existing official and alternative Android markets. DroidMOSS [76] uses *fuzzy hashing* to detect repackaged apps in third-party Android marketplaces. DroidScope [73] reconstructs the semantic views of the OS and Dalvik for dynamic Android malware analysis.

Chapter 6
Summary

In this book, we present an overview of existing Android malware and further systematically characterize their behavior from different perspectives. The characterization is made possible with our more than one-year effort in collecting 1260 Android malware samples in 49 different families, which covers the majority of existing Android malware, ranging from its debut in August 2010 to the end of 2011. By characterizing these malware samples from various aspects, our results show that (1) 86.0 % of them repackage legitimate apps to include malicious payloads; (2) 36.7 % contain platform-level exploits to escalate privilege; (3) 93.0 % communicate with remote servers and/or exhibit bot-like functionality. A further in-depth evolution analysis of representative Android malware shows the rapid development and increased sophistication, posing significant challenges for their detection. As existing mobile security solutions still lag behind, these results call for the need to better develop next-generation anti-mobile-malware solutions.

X. Jiang and Y. Zhou, *Android Malware*, SpringerBriefs in Computer Science,
DOI: 10.1007/978-1-4614-7394-7_6, © The Author(s) 2013

References

1. Acm, CCS Workshop on Security and Privacy in Smartphones and Mobile Devices. http://www.spsm-workshop.org/
2. ACM Conference on Computer and Communications Security. http://www.sigsac.org/ccs.html
3. Adb Trickery #2. http://c-skills.blogspot.com/2011/01/adb-trickery-again.html
4. An Analysis of the AnserverBot Trojan. http://www.csc.ncsu.edu/faculty/jiang/pubs/Anserver Bot_Analysis.pdf
5. Android Trickery. http://c-skills.blogspot.com/2010/07/android-trickery.html
6. Android. Bgserv Found on Fake Google Security Patch. http://www.symantec.com/connect/blogs/androidbgserv-found-fake-google-security-patch
7. Asroot. http://milw0rm.com/sploits/android-root-20090816.tar.gz
8. AVG Mobilation. http://free.avg.com/us-en/antivirus-for-android.tpl-crp
9. Droid2. http://c-skills.blogspot.com/2010/08/droid2.html
10. DroidKungFu Utilizes an Update Attack. http://www.f-secure.com/weblog/archives/00002259.html
11. "Fee-Deduction" Malware Targeting Android Devices Spotted in the Wild. http://www.securityweek.com/fee-deduction-malware-targeting-android-devices-spotted-wild
12. First SpyEye Attack on Android Mobile Platform now in the Wild. https://www.trusteer.com/blog/first-spyeye-attack-android-mobile-platform-now-wild
13. Fortinet. http://www.fortinet.com/
14. GGTracker Technical Tear Down. http://blog.mylookout.com/wp-content/uploads/2011/06/GGTracker-Teardown_Lookout-Mobile-Security.pdf
15. IEEE Symposium on Security and Privacy. http://www.ieee-security.org/TC/SP-Index.html
16. Lookout Mobile Security. https://www.mylookout.com/
17. Malicious Mobile Threats Report 2010/2011. http://www.juniper.net/us/en/company/press-center/press-releases/2011/pr_2011_05_10-09_00.html
18. Malicious QR Codes Pushing Android Malware. https://www.securelist.com/en/blog/208193145/Its_time_for_malicious_QR_codes
19. Mobile Security Technologies. http://www.spsm-workshop.org/
20. NDSS Symposium. http://www.internetsociety.org/events/ndss-symposium
21. NetQin Mobile Security. http://www.netqin.com/en/
22. Number of the Week: at Least 34% of Android Malware Is Stealing Your Data. http://www.kaspersky.com/about/news/virus/2011/Number_of_the_Week_at_Least_34_of_Android_Malware_Is_Stealing_Your_Data
23. One Year Of Android Malware (Full List). http://paulsparrows.wordpress.com/2011/08/11/one-year-of-android-malware-full-list/
24. QR code. http://en.wikipedia.org/wiki/QR_code
25. Remote Kill and Install on Google Android. http://jon.oberheide.org/blog/2010/06/25/remote-kill-and-install-on-google-android/

X. Jiang and Y. Zhou, *Android Malware*, SpringerBriefs in Computer Science,
DOI: 10.1007/978-1-4614-7394-7, © The Author(s) 2013

26. Revolutionary - zergRush Local Root 2.2/2.3. http://forum.xda-developers.com/show thread.php?t=1296916
27. Security Alert: AnserverBot, New Sophisticated Android Bot Found in Alternative Android Markets. http://www.csc.ncsu.edu/faculty/jiang/AnserverBot/
28. Security Alert: First Android SMS Trojan Found in the Wild. http://blog. mylookout.com/2010/08/security-alert-first-android-sms-trojan-found-in-the-wild/
29. Security Alert: New DroidKungFu Variant - AGAIN! - Found in Alternative Android Markets. http://www.csc.ncsu.edu/faculty/jiang/DroidKungFu3/
30. Security Alert: New Stealthy Android Spyware - Plankton - Found in Official Android Market. http://www.csc.ncsu.edu/faculty/jiang/Plankton/
31. Symantec. http://www.symantec.com/
32. TrendMicro. http://www.virustotal.com/
33. USENIX Security Symposium. https://www.usenix.org/conferences/byname/108
34. Using QR tags to Attack SmartPhones (Attaging). http://kaoticoneutral.blogspot.com/2011/09/using-qr-tags-to-attack-smartphones_10.html
35. WAPS. http://www.waps.cn/
36. Yummy Yummy, GingerBreak! http://c-skills.blogspot.com/2011/04/yummy-yummy-ginger break.html
37. ZeuS-in-the-Mobile - Facts and Theories. http://www.securelist.com/en/analysis/204792194/ZeuS_in_the_Mobile_Facts_and_Theories
38. Zimperlich sources. http://c-skills.blogspot.com/2011/02/zimperlich-sources.html
39. Smartphone Shipments Tripled Since '08. Dumb Phones Are Flat. http://tech. fortune.cnn.com/2011/11/01/smartphone-shipments-tripled-since-08-dumb-phones-are-flat, 2011.
40. J. Andrus, C. Dall, A. Van't Hof, O. Laadan, J. Nieh, Cells: A virtual mobile smartphone architecture. in Proceedings of the 23rd ACM Symposium on Operating Systems Principles, 2011.
41. A.R. Beresford, A. Rice, N. Skehin, R. Sohan, MockDroid: Trading privacy for application functionality on smartphones. in Proceedings of the 12th International Workshop on Mobile Computing System and Applications, 2011.
42. S. Bugiel, L. Davi, A. Dmitrienko, T. Fischer, A.-R. Sadeghi, B. Shastry, Towards taming privilege-escalation attacks on android. in Proceedings of the 19th Annual Symposium on Network and Distributed System, Security, 2012.
43. E. Chin, A.P. Felt, K. Greenwood, D. Wagner, Analyzing inter-application communication in android. in 9th Annual International Conference on Mobile Systems, Applications, and Services, 2011.
44. M. Christodorescu, S. Jha, D. Maughan, D. Song, C. Wang, *Malware Defense* (Springer, New York, 2006).
45. C. Collberg, J. Nagra, *Surreptitious software: obfuscation, watermarking, and tamperproofing for software protection* (Addison-Wesley Professional, Boston, 2009).
46. M. Dietz, S. Shekhar, Y. Pisetsky, A. Shu, D.S. Wallach, QUIRE: lightweight provenance for smart phone operating systems. in Proceedings of the 20th USENIX Security, Symposium, 2011.
47. K. Dunham, *Mobile Malware Attacks and Defense* (Syngress, Boston, 2008).
48. H. Dwivedi, C. Clark, D. Thiel, *Mobile Application Security* (Mc Graw Hill, New York, 2010).
49. M. Egele, C. Kruegel, E. Kirda, G. Vigna, PiOS: detecting privacy leaks in iOS applications. in Proceedings of the 18th Annual Symposium on Network and Distributed System, Security, 2011.
50. W. Enck, P. Gilbert, B.-g. Chun, L.P. Cox, J. Jung, P. McDaniel, A.N. Sheth, TaintDroid: an information-flow tracking system for realtime privacy monitoring on smartphones. in Proceedings of the 9th USENIX Symposium on Operating Systems Design and Implementation, 2010.

51. W. Enck, M. Ongtang, P. McDaniel, On lightweight mobile phone application certification. in Proceedings of the 16th ACM Conference on Computer and Communications, Security, 2009.
52. A.P. Felt, E. Chin, S. Hanna, D. Song, D. Wagner, Android permissions demystied. in Proceedings of the 18th ACM Conference on Computer and Communications, Security, 2011.
53. A.P. Felt, M. Finifter, E. Chin, S. Hanna, D. Wagner, A survey of mobile malware in the wild. in Proceedings of the 1st Workshop on Security and Privacy in Smartphones and Mobile Devices, 2011.
54. A.P. Felt, H.J. Wang, A. Moshchuk, S. Hanna, E. Chin, Permission re-delegation: attacks and defenses. in Proceedings of the 20th USENIX Security, Symposium, 2011.
55. M. Grace, W. Zhou, X. Jiang, A.-R. Sadeghi, Unsafe exposure analysis of mobile In-App advertisements. in Proceedings of the 5th ACM Conference on Security and Privacy in Wireless and Mobile, Networks, 2012.
56. M. Grace, Y. Zhou, Z. Wang, X. Jiang, Systematic detection of capability leaks in stock android smartphones. in Proceedings of the 19th Annual Symposium on Network and Distributed System, Security, 2012.
57. M. Grace, Y. Zhou, Q. Zhang, S. Zou, X. Jiang, RiskRanker: scalable and accurate zero-day android malware detection. in Proceedings of the 10th International Conference on Mobile Systems, Applications and Services, 2012.
58. N. Hardy, The Confused Deputy: (or why capabilities might have been invented). in ACM SIGOPS Operating Systems, Review, 22 Oct 1998.
59. A. Hoog, *Android Forensics: Investigation, Analysis and Mobile Security for Google Android* (Syngress, Waltham, 2011).
60. A. Hoog, K. Strzempka, *iPhone and iOS Forensics: Investigation, Analysis and Mobile Security for Apple iPhone, iPad and iOS Devices* (Syngress, Waltham, 2011).
61. P. Hornyack, S. Han, J. Jung, S. Schechter, D. Wetherall, These aren't the droids you're looking for: retrofitting android to protect data from imperious applications. in Proceedings of the 18th ACM Conference on Computer and Communications, Security, 2011.
62. M. Lange, S. Liebergeld, A. Lackorzynski, A. Warg, M. Peter, L4Android: a generic operating system framework for secure smartphones. in Proceedings of the 1st Workshop on Security and Privacy in Smartphones and Mobile Devices, 2011.
63. W. Lee, C. Wang, D. Dagon, *Botnet Detection* (Springer, New York, 2008).
64. M. Masud, L. Khan, B. Thuraisingham, *Data Mining Tools for Malware Detection* (CRC Press, London, 2011).
65. E. Metula, *Managed Code Rootkits: Hooking into Runtime Environments* (Syngress, Burlington, 2010).
66. M. Nauman, S. Khan, X. Zhang, Apex: extending android permission model and enforcement with user-defined runtime constraints. in Proceedings of the 5th ACM Symposium on Information, Computer and Communications, Security, 2010.
67. M. Ongtang, S. McLaughlin, W. Enck, P. McDaniel, Semantically rich application-centric security in android. in Proceedings of the 25th Annual Computer Security Applications Conference, 2009.
68. S. Schrittwieser, P. Frhwirt, P. Kieseberg, M. Leithner, M. Mulazzani, M. Huber, E. Weippl, Guess who's texting you? evaluating the security of smartphone messaging applications. in Proceedings of the 19th Annual Symposium on Network and Distributed System, Security, 2012.
69. S. Shekhar, M. Dietz, D.S. Wallach, AdSplit: separating smartphone advertising from applications. in Proceedings of the 21th USENIX Security, Symposium, 2012.
70. C. Silvio, X. Yang, *Software Similarity and Classification* (Springer, New York, 2012).
71. P. Traynor, M. Lin, M. Ongtang, V. Rao, T. Jaeger, P. McDaniel, T.L. Porta, On cellular botnets: measuring the impact of malicious devices on a cellular network core. in Proceedings of the 16th ACM Conference on Computer and Communications, Security, 2009.

72. R. Xu, H. Saidi, R. Anderson, Aurasium: practical policy enforcement for android applications. in Proceedings of the 21th USENIX Security, Symposium, 2012.
73. L.K. Yan, H. Yin, DroidScope: seamlessly reconstructing the OS and Dalvik semantic views for dynamic android malware analysis. in Proceedings of the 21th USENIX Security, Symposium, 2012.
74. H. Yin, D. Song, *Automatic Malware Analysis: An Emulator based Approach* (Springer, New York, 2013).
75. J. Zdziarski, *Hacking and Securing iOS Applications: Stealing Data, Hijacking Software, and How to Prevent It* (O'Reilly, Media, Sebastopol, 2012).
76. W. Zhou, Y. Zhou, X. Jiang, P. Ning, DroidMOSS: detecting repackaged smartphone applications in third-party android marketplaces. in Proceedings of the 2nd ACM Conference on Data and Application Security and Privacy, 2012.
77. Y. Zhou, X. Jiang, Dissecting android malware: characterization and evolution. in Proceedings of the 33nd IEEE Symposium on Security and Privacy, 2012.
78. Y. Zhou, Z. Wang, W. Zhou, X. Jiang, Hey, you, get off of my market: detecting malicious apps in official and alternative android markets. in Proceedings of the 19th Annual Symposium on Network and Distributed System, Security, 2012.
79. Y. Zhou, X. Zhang, X. Jiang, V.W. Freeh, Taming information-stealing smartphone applications (on android). in Proceeding of the 4th International Conference on Trust and Trustworthy, Computing, 2011.

Index

X. Jiang and Y. Zhou, *Android Malware*, SpringerBriefs in Computer Science,
DOI: 10.1007/978-1-4614-7394-7, © The Author(s) 2013